A LIFETIME KIND OF LOVE

GWYNETH LESLEY

OUTSPOKEN INK PRESS

OUTSPOKEN INK PRESS

First published in New Zealand in 2022 by Outspoken Ink Press

Text copyright © Gwyneth Lesley, 2022
Cover image copyright © Gram Telen
Interior illustrations: Zela © Gwyneth Lesley
Interior formatting © Gram Telen
Editor: Sarina Cornthwaite
Author image: © Johanna Elizabeth, 2020

The moral rights of the author and
illustrators have been asserted.

A catalogue record for this book is available
from the New Zealand Library.

PRINT ISBN: 978-0-473-62356-2
EBOOK ISBN: 978-0-473-62358-6

THE FEMME FATALE SERIES BOOK #2: A LIFETIME KIND OF LOVE

One for sorrow
Two for joy
Three for a girl
Four for a boy
Five for silver
Six for gold
Seven for a secret never to be told.

Seven women agreed to tell you
their stories in this series.

The first, Amara, you may have met in book one,
Prometheus' Priestess.

This is not a continuation of her tale.
Though, along with the other women,
she will reappear together in sisterhood
as this series progresses.

You will find the answers you seek... eventually.
These women, in turn, will ask questions of you
that you must be willing to seek
the answers to yourself.

For how can you write a new ending
to your story, humanity,
if you aren't willing to look at the myths?

The distortions.
The deceit.
The misfortune.

This is not a series where you will
be spoon-fed the answers.
These women have no interest in
telling you lullabies & fairytales
for you to escape into anymore.

Not when your world is crumbling.

You are the messengers through
which their words travel.
It's up to you to unravel them.

You walk alongside them,
but you haven't been listening.

Until now.

It's time to tell you our story again.

OTHER BOOKS IN THIS SERIES

PROMETHEUS' PRIESTESS

PRAISE FOR THE AUTHOR

"A fantasy romance that will sweep you off your feet before crashing back down to Earth as it delves into the human condition with staggering accuracy." – Jessica Kate

"She's got such magic in her bones and it bleeds onto the paper." – Pippa Leslie

"So well done with bringing in old and ancient histories with a modern setting. The author blends the two worlds perfectly." – Taylor

"Definitely recommend to people who have never read any Greek mythology and are looking to expand their reading palette." – Jessica Hollister

"There were so many lessons throughout the book that made me sit back and reflect on my personal life/purpose on Earth." – Erica

Archetypes: universal, primal symbols and images that derive from the collective unconscious.

The Lovers: those who live for intimacy & relationships; who would rather risk losing their identity in the one they love than end up alone.

From the Greek *arkhetupon*: something moulded first as a model.

THE TALE OF HADES &
PERSEPHONE

Before we begin, let me introduce you to the lineage of Hades & Persephone, particularly for those of you unfamiliar with Greek mythology.

It's been said that Hades, God of the Underworld and brother of Zeus, on one of the rare times he left the underworld, saw a fair maiden roaming the earth and fell in love with her. That maiden was Persephone, daughter of Demeter; the Goddess of the Harvest. Hades asked for help from Zeus to kidnap Persephone, and so, one day, when she was playing in the fields with her companions, the ground beneath her feet split. She slid into the underworld where Hades made her his wife.

Demeter, distraught at losing her daughter, asked the nearby nymphs who had been close to Persephone where she was. They had no answer, so she cursed them into those we know today as the sirens. A dutiful mother, Demeter continued to search the earth for Persephone – forgetting her harvest duties. In this way, famine became personified, too.

Eventually, it was revealed that Persephone had been taken to the underworld.

As Demeter demanded her daughter back, Hades slipped Persephone four pomegranate seeds, which she ate. To eat the fruit of one's captor meant one would have to return to their captor's side. And so, Persephone, whether willingly or not, was tied to the bind of the pomegranate seeds. In order to quieten Demeter's demands, and return the earth to a time before famine, Zeus decreed that Persephone must split her time between Earth and the underworld, to keep each bond - to Hades and to Demeter - satisfied.

When she returns to her mother, spring emerges. And when she descends to Hades, autumn is upon us.

Now you know the tale of Hades and Persephone. Or do you? What about that blink of time when they both roamed the earth? The myth says it was but a moment, but what is a moment to an immortal if not a lifetime to a mortal?

This collection of poetry explores what that mortal time on Earth looked like for these two lovers. And while this can be enjoyed as a retelling of their story – or, rather, a tale that hasn't been told at all before, when they are both in mortal form on the earth – it can also simply be enjoyed as a collection of love notes to peruse at your leisure.

OTHER GODS,
GODDESSES & DEITIES
IT MAY HELP TO KNOW

ZEUS
God of Gods.

MOIRAI
The three sisters otherwise known as The Fates.

STYX
The river of the underworld. The gods swear by her water as their most binding oath.

ARES
God of war, violence, male virility, and defender of the weak.

LILITH
Not a Greek Goddess, but a Babylonian demonic creature if literature is to be believed, Lilith represents the dark shadow of a woman's rebellious independence that has been shunned by society.

ERIS
The personification of strife, who relishes in bloodshed. Daughter of Nyx (Night) and sister of Ares.

ICARUS
The son of Daedalus – a master craftsman who built them both wings made of wax and feathers to escape Crete. Icarus ignored his father's instructions not to fly too close to the sun and his wings melted. He tumbled out of the sky, fell into the sea and drowned.

CHRONOS
God of time.

CALYPSO
Goddess-nymph of the mythical island of Ogygia, known for her strange power and beauty that kept mortal men captive.

HESTIA
Goddess of hearth and home.

TYCHE
Goddess of fortune and chance.

APHRODITE
Goddess of love, beauty, passion, and procreation.

SISYPHUS
An old Greek King who has been eternally punished by Hades for cheating death twice. He is forced to roll an immense boulder up a hill only for it to roll down every time it nears the top, repeating this action for eternity.

CHARON
Ferryman of Hades. Carries souls of the newly deceased who have received the rites of burial across the river Styx.

ATHENA
Goddess of wisdom and war. Known for mentoring young heroes in times of challenge. Here it appears she offers the same favour to our heroine.

GAIA
The personification of the earth, and one of the Greek primordial deities, aka Mother Earth.

ARTEMIS
Goddess of wild animals, the hunt, vegetation, and of chastity and childbirth. Twin sister of Apollo.

APOLLO
God of the sun and light, music and poetry, healing and plagues, prophecy and knowledge, order and beauty, archery and agriculture. Twin brother of Artemis.

AUTHOR'S NOTE

When I began writing this book, I had no idea that it would become a self-fulfilling prophecy. I almost regret writing the words "I'd go to hell and back for you," because that is exactly what I did.

I do not like to romanticise a creative suffering for their work, and I don't believe it has to be the case. In fact, I felt pure joy writing the first book, *Prometheus' Priestess*. Picking it up to read, every time is still a joy for me.

This book, however, quite literally almost killed me. I began writing it on July 12th of 2021 and by August 21st, I was full-blown suicidal. I do not say this for pity or attention, but as a warning and a disclaimer. If you are in a bad place mentally right now, I would invite you to pick up this book another time.

Initially, these poems were pulled from a past love who had reappeared briefly in this lifetime with a connection that floored both of us with its strength and brutality. But over time, as the poems pulled from deeper and darker places of me, places I didn't even know existed, I realised that all of the poems – even the ones I believed were for him – were all love letters to me. From my soul to my human form. *The whole time*. Which is why you'll often come across rhetorical questions that answer themselves between one stanza and the next in these poems. Each poem was as much an internal conversation as it was an external mirroring, as all archetypes are.

The loves that appear in our lifetimes are simply mirrors. They are, more often than not, designed to crack us open to love we did not know we could hold, until that moment.

In my mind, there is no shadow of a doubt why the ancestries of Persephone & Hades chose to present themselves for this book. The archetypes of lovers, as well as King & Queen in the form of life & death, were brutal companions on this journey. But their story is as beautiful as it is heartbreaking.

And I have always maintained that heartbreak is a beautiful thing. That the cracking of a heart allows more love in, that tears are the husk of a heart hardened to life, melting away. But that does not make for light reading. In fact, it often requires us to go to the darkest parts of ourselves, parts that are uncomfortable, confronting and, in my case, can make us question our nature, if we are worthy of love (and therefore, life), and how to break the shackles that chain us to the belief we are not. To love through grief in both life and in death, for grief is merely love that hasn't learnt to let go yet.

And how do you grieve something that has never come to fruition? Something that was never quite formed enough to be considered "alive," but was formed *enough* to have been more than just mere thought. Women who have experienced miscarriage will understand this concept, even if they cannot put it into words. It's possibly why some of the Mother/ Maiden theme slips into these pages too.

It is certainly present in Demeter & Persephone's dynamic, another reason why the tale had to be told through this lineage. For the grief that forms not only through love and fruition, but also that which rears its head from abandonment, is as all-consuming, albeit in a much subtler subconscious simmering.

Experiences like this, be it an unborn child, a love that never reaches full potential, an idea that never quite makes it to fruition, exist in a sort of purgatory we often don't acknowledge. That is where I found myself during the months writing this book – purgatory. There was no colour, no life. The lockdowns of 2020 & 2021 had sucked the little tolerance in humanity out. I had little tolerance in my own humanity. And yet, in the darkest moments, I was reminded that life on Earth is all three: heaven, hell, and purgatory. It's whichever one you choose.

If you fill it full of life and wonder, you will experience heaven on Earth. The hiccup of your heart when your lover takes your hand for the first time. The jolt of lightning you get when your eyes first meet. The longing and the heartbreak that makes the wait worth it. The smell of cookies baking in the kitchen.

You can choose to make it hell, taking bitter advice and seeing everyone or everything as out to get you. You can blame your family for the template they gave you, rather than taking radical responsibility. You can feel hard done by, abandoned, taken advantage of.

And sometimes, you simply stop seeing the colour of the world. If heaven is the white space we are free to fill with wonder, and hell is the black border lines to give us order, then purgatory is where we find our shading. Should you choose to shade everything grey then, of course, oblivion will look more appealing. But should you choose to fill it with colour, you know that those moments of hell simply give shape and perspective to the freedom you are experiencing. For shape gives us space to create, to take responsibility, to make judgements and choices. And therein lies your path to heaven on Earth: the choices you make.

The dead lovers is a tale that, like the rest in the Femme Fatale series, is filled with sorrow yet joy, a girl and a boy, elements of the earth and a secret understanding many of us know but aren't often able to put into words; that you can find joy even in the shades of grey in which grief presents itself. And when you do, then even death is Heaven-bound.

To T, for your nudge in every lifetime.

*And to Tom, for your unfailing
friendship in this one.*

TABLE OF CONTENTS

PRELUDE TO HUMANITY

The Untold Tale Of Hades 35
Welcome To The Abyss 36
Garden Of Eden 39
Perfectly Scarred 40
Hades & Persephone 41

FIRE & FIGHT

Bonfire. 46
Quiet Whispers. 48
In The Sacred Temple 49
Road Trips With The Carpenter 51
The Wisdom Of The Fool. 53
With Thy Body, I Thee Worship 55
Let Us Sink Into Sin. 56
Disguise. 60
Honeybee 62
"You're Loved.". 64
A Seat At The Table 66
Empty Promises 68

Martyrdom 71

Purpose 73

Advice To Persephone From

   Fellow Goddesses 75

Synonymous 79

And So The Rebirth Begins... 80

Lean In 81

The Sacred Whore 82

Grant Me Peace 84

Perhaps You Should Pray 85

Icarus' Ancestor 87

WATER & RELEASE

Held 90

Blackbirds 91

The Siren Call 92

Another Lifetime 94

Reflections 96

Slivers 97

Alone 99

A Woman Of The World 100

The Fisherwoman 103

Persephone And Demeter 104

That God Damned Dinghy Boat 106

Cancer Season 109

North Node 111
The God, The Girl & The Fisherwoman 113
The Scales Of Libra 114
Practice 117
Under The Mountain 118

EARTH & ABSENCE

The Forest Of Futures Past 123
Hide 127
The Wrong Sacrifice 129
A Message From Eris 130
Appetite 131
Honestly 132
The Antidote 133
Nowhere 134
Tyche's Stalemate 135
Every Inch 137
Nowhere Is Where You Need To Go 138
Nothing To Stand For 140
Disciplina 141
Desire 142
Persephone's Cauldron .144
Lessons 146

AIR & SKIN

Befriending Death 149

Persephone To Hades 151

Heroin 153

Madness Seeped In 154

Hades To Persephone 155

Hurricane 156

Marked 158

Goodbyes. 160

Heartbreak 161

This Sinking Feeling 162

Demon Fodder 163

The Council Of The Inner Woman 165

Company To Keep 166

Athena To Persephone. 168

Moments 169

Dust On The Wind 170

So Say The Greek Playwrights 171

And Perhaps... 172

Bargaining With Angels. 173

From Maiden To Mother. 174

Angels 177

UNDERWORLD

When The Dead Talk 181

A Seat With The Gods 183

"Mama, Why Don't We Go To Church
   On Sundays?" 185

Epilogue: Melancholy 189

Melinoë 191

Femme Fatale 192

Acknowledgements 193

PRELUDE TO HUMANITY

THE UNTOLD TALE OF HADES

When her small delicate hand
Reached for mine
Pulled the purpose from my throat
With her tongue
Wrapped her divinity around me
And demanded my soul...

I walked the earth again,
for her.

They say I pursued her.
Chased her.
Hounded her.

All I did was love her
With reckless abandon
For that was the only way she knew
How to love herself.

WELCOME TO THE ABYSS

Roll up, roll up,
Liquor up.
Get your pick and mix of drugs
Pick at cotton candy heartache
As you peruse the fun.

You, sir, yes you!
Is violence your kink?
Try the school ride.
The kids are inside.
Don't forget the gun.

Bumper cars? Try bumping lives.
Throw glass against the wall.
Better yet, why not beat a woman
Inside those four walls?

Take a ticket
Join the ride
Step into the abyss.

Roll up, roll up
World's strongest man
Take all the burdens for yourself

Let's see how long it takes, shall we folks,
To crush his mental health?

Don't cry little girl,
Here, take a Love-Me-Not.

It'll rot your insides
But besides,
You must be deeply insecure
To enter the house of mirrors
And lose yourself forevermore.

Paint a clown smile on your face.
There, aren't you prettier my dear?

Take a ticket
Join the ride
Step into the abyss.

Roll up, roll up
Pick your poison
Choose a wound.

You'll never need to leave
This glorious place of doom and gloom.

Roll up, roll up
Demons & deities
The humans are at your mercy.
For all your wants and needs.

Let's give a hand
to those humans,
For being such
good killing sports.

Who knew they had such a knack?

Pick a mask
Come masquerade on Earth

Watch the freak show act.

GARDEN OF EDEN

I would pick you.
An odd thing to say
For you are not a flower,
But a bramble bush.

With history and gnarled roots
And thorns that prick at my thumbs.

Yet, I would pick you nonetheless.

That is not to say I would uproot you.
I would leave you in your garden.

For why take you from nourishment
And place that burden on myself?

Far rather
That I shower you
With love and adoration
From this spot in the garden,
Knowing that I have picked you
Without taking you from your home.

-

Hades to Persephone's mortal form

PERFECTLY SCARRED

Beautiful things don't ask for attention.
Beautiful minds don't need direction.

And beautiful people, rare as they are
Aren't always perfect, but perfectly scarred.

HADES & PERSEPHONE

In the first decade,
In the seventh year,
The Gods gifted me pain.

A body sacrifice.
An initiation into war.
An invitation into wisdom.

Ten years of blood-soaked battlefields, my love.
Of dirt-covered demons
Stitching pieces of my soul back together.

Until, in the second decade,
In the seventh year,
The Gods gifted me grace.

A blood rite of passage
A baby boy
Not to be born,
But a promise made on knees
Hardened on bathroom tiles
Of the woman I would be
Come to earth.

A reclaiming.

And suddenly, there you were.
In the doorway. On your knees with me.
Covered in the same dirt that clung to me.
Covered in the same blood I'd spilled.
That haunted look in your eyes
That said you knew my demons better than I.

In the second decade,
In the seventh year,
On the sixth month,
The Gods gifted me you.

And suddenly it all made sense.
Like how you know the sky is blue.

Except the seasons have stopped.
The sun no longer rises or sets.
The winds no longer howl.

And yet there is chaos all around us.
The eye of the storm
Brutal and unblinking
You watch me warily
As if you're worried I'm a mirage
A cunning trick from Moirai.

So used you are to pain, my love.

I hand you hard-earned coins.
For safe passage, I say.
For you swim in Styx's water so easily.
And swear oaths that could get you killed.

So used you are to battle, my love.

You hand me a sweet pomegranate seed.
An everlasting Queendom, you offer.
For hope springs eternal
And our souls are immortal.

And I realise, in that moment,
I'd walk to hell and back all over again.
My feet bare and burnished black
For you.

And I wonder,
When the mortals talk of love stories,
If they realise
Hades & Persephone walk among them.

FIRE & FIGHT

When the need for love is too great, we
often find the mortals over-give.
Placing pressure on the other, they grow angry
when their unsolicited offerings are rejected.

BONFIRE

A flickering of recognition
Against flames
That dance in eyesight.

I have seen you
On this beach

Before.

That build,
That muscle,
That hair,

That wounded wisdom,
That jaw of pride,
And those sad eyes.

Oh, I have seen those eyes before.

Come
Step into the bonfire,
Burnt earth tastes a little sweeter.

Let it burn away every trauma,
Every untrue belief you've ever told.
Let the entirety of your ego
Turn to little more than ash.

I can work with that.

Ah... exposure scares you.
Knowledge even more.

For who would you be
If the fire between us
Stripped away
Everything you are not?

Come
Step into the bonfire,
Burnt earth tastes a little sweeter.

We've been burnt before.

QUIET WHISPERS

The quiet whispers in a temple
are far more potent
than the cries on the street.

For it is the beauty of mystery
that attracts us.

IN THE SACRED TEMPLE

The thing about desperate men
Is that they are duty bound by pressure
To succeed, unfortunately
It takes away all pleasure.

So we strip them of that first
When they enter the halls of sacred temptation.
The need to please
And succeed.

But there was no air of desperation
When you entered through those doors,
Just pure exhaustion.

And so I stripped you of tired leathers,
You, a battle-weary warrior,
And I bathed with you in salted waters
Filled with the silent tears
Many men had shed before.
Yours joined them.

Afterwards, I rested your head in my lap
Luxuriating in the heavy weight of it,

The thickness of your curls
Tangled through my fingers
As you spoke of horrors you would not
Take home to your wife
And transcribed them into lullabies
Of heroic tales
You'd be proud to tell your daughter
One day.

How I wish we still lived in those times,
With those temples
Where warrior's wounds were soothed
By women who understood
The rites of passage men like you
Willingly walked into.

How I long to return to the first lifetime we met.

ROAD TRIPS WITH THE CARPENTER

Let passion be the starting point
For humans know no better,
He tells me.

Let passion be the fuel, the spark, the fire.

Let passion be the door breaking open ajar
Let passion be your drive & your desire.

For even fury has a starting point
A flickering of flame
To a purpose and a path
A cause with no name.

But as you lean into the lesson
learning what new realms of love exist,
Do not mistake the dousing
For entrenchment.

Rather,
Look upon the language
See dowsing as a gift
Designed to drench
You in the love
That will always
Exist.

THE WISDOM OF THE FOOL

I laid out the puzzle pieces of my heart
Covered in protective film
To see how you would handle them.

Too many people
Had thumbed the originals,
Smudged the colouring
From red to battered pink.

I gave you those well-worn pieces first
To see what you would do with them.

You held them gently.
Laid them down.
Asked for more.

So I gave you the edges next.
Then the odd pieces.
The ones which didn't seem to fit
In a picture that didn't make sense.

The strangest thing...

You managed to piece them all together
And peel back the protective film.

It's beautiful, you said.
Then you began to break it down.

If nothing breaks, nothing moves.

So you began to build it anew
Creating a space just for you.

WITH THY BODY, I THEE WORSHIP

Let me love you
Now, like in lifetimes past.

With thy body
In worship,
Hallowed by your touch.
An intertwining like no other
A remembering all at once.

LET US SINK INTO SIN

Your body heat behind me,
I've never felt so secure

Rough calluses kiss my shoulders
Your lips peruse my neck

It has been many moons, my love
Since we have done this.

Come, wrap yourself around me
Let us sink into sin.

Wait, let me love you first.

A curve of breast,
A slow, wet suckle
A breath of hot air.

A kiss of teeth
Across soft creamy flesh

Your tongue
Lavishes new scores

A flash of eye contact
Sears me to my core.

A glint of promise
And a grin against skin
Holds divine retribution.

A pathway made
With soft lips

To the cradle
where it all began

You prepare
A sweet feast, a ravishing

Circling the seven levels of Hell
To touch the tip of ecstasy

Now.

Wait, let me love you first.

A weightlessness
A wall

A desperate need
To claim

Broken
Only by breathlessness

The sweet torture
Of the wait
The break

The promise
Of more to -

Come, wrap yourself around me
Let us sink into sin.

Oh dear, I am eternally damned.

DISGUISE

If I place rose petals on your eyelids
And adorn myself in accolades,

If I smile sweetly at your laugh
And soften at your harshness,

If I wrap temptation and domesticity
In the folds of my skin,

And whisper words of affection
While silently cursing your demons

Perhaps you will see the purity
Of a heart I do not trust you to hold.

Perhaps then,
You will wear
Safety
Security
Compassion
And comfort
In the folds of your chain mail
Confidently.

And offer to house my heart
Behind a steel breastplate
Made of blood and bone.

Yet, for some reason,
I'm fairly certain
Even that disguise won't save me.

HONEYBEE

Here my love, have some honey
Drip down your throat.

Just a taste.

Savour the sweetness on
This silver spoon I offer.

Don't push back. Don't resist.
This is ambrosia to the Gods.

No?
No more?
You're certain?

How can you be so ungrateful?

For this collection of nectar
I have poured over.

Oh.

You cannot stomach
A steady stream
And now you're choking.

That stings.

"YOU'RE LOVED."

The subtlety of an apostrophe.
For all mistake it for present tense
But that's just pretence
Isn't it, my love?

For we exist
in the past
present
and future.

But you
were not referring to now.
How could you be?

For you do not feel safe to be seen
With eyes that see through façades.

You do not feel worthy
Of love you have not earned.

You cannot even be grateful
For the presence of presents
With which you are gifted.
I can see it, for I once walked that same path
Of pre-sense.

Instead, you present yourself a man with purpose.
Yet your cause, to you, remains unknown.

And isn't that the catch?

For until you find it
You will forever have me in your past
And in your future.
But never in your present.

"You're loved."
Imagine that.

A SEAT AT THE TABLE

"Will He come?"

The Mother shrugs
cradling the Maiden closer.

"Whether He does or not,
we have a heart to stew."

The others
around the table
offer their opinions.

He comes... to play.
He comes... to devour.
He comes... I am watching.
He comes.

And you?
What say you,
wise woman?

"The question
is not whether He comes, my child.

The question
is do you lay a place for Him?"

EMPTY PROMISES

You broke your word.
All the other things I can forgive,
But not that.

Never that.

Empty promises of the man
You will one day become
Are just that...

Empty
Pretty
Words

Shattered at my feet like glass.

Shards of heartbreak prick at my heels
As ancestral blood bears footprints on the floor
Leading me to you.

Your nostrils flare
And I can't quite tell if you are baying for blood

Or for the liquor that was once held in those
    Empty glass promises of yours.

No matter,
You'll deny both, if it will keep you
    In the Kingdom.

If it will keep you a King.

I watch you claim a title you don't own
    A teaching you cannot embody

And I watch them praise you for it.

Tell me,
While you're busy shepherding sheep
Who is shepherding you,
Who has forsaken all who would
    Offer a true hand of hope?

Even Kings require counsel.

Instead you issue commands
    More empty words
    As if I am not an Oracle.

As if the reflection I offer you
Is not stained in bloodied glass.

As if wine cannot be turned back to water,
As if you cannot be turned back to truth.

But I weave words
In a way designed to leave you craving more.

Because I know the power of
A sweet kiss of promise
Come true.

MARTYRDOM

Who are you to tell me
What I can hold in my heart?

Who are you to dictate a woman's desires?

Are your bones dipped that deep in Patriarchy
That you wage war on a woman's
Right to choose?

Even now,
With her beating heart between you?

Here you are, self-sacrificing.
Falling on your sword for the greater good.

Blunt knives like yours need a little
more blunt force trauma.

Don't you know Zeus despises sacrifices
of human flesh?

Don't you know claiming martyrdom
without good cause
is merely cowardice claiming nobility?

There is nothing noble
in throwing away
opportunities
Gifted from the Gods.

Disguising demons
as excuses for escape
with good intention
is not good cause.

Yet, here you stand

A coward
who stakes his claim
on the crumbling ruins
of martyrdom.

Claiming victory
In a war you cannot possibly win.

PURPOSE

I never wanted a production made
Out of loving me.

Forced effort on your part
I was supposed to applaud
While feeling like a chore.

All I wanted

Was your presence
Alongside me.

You cannot find what you refuse to look for.

ADVICE TO PERSEPHONE
FROM FELLOW GODDESSES

We, the two who walk beside Ares
We, Lilith and Eris,
Deliver the dead to your beloved King.

He, who does not do the dirty work
Of digging his hands into soiled souls
To pull out dead roots.

Oh, he says he does
But then why, oh Daughter of Demeter,
Does hell hath no fury like a *woman* scorned?

You, who have never known
Scorched earth unless it is sweet.

You have never known
Earth while it bathes
In the blood of men who battle their true nature.

See how Eris licks her blade,
Relishing in it?
That is because men stripped her
Of manipulation and claimed it
As their own.

See how they cower from Lilith
Once she seeks payment for
The warmth she offered them
Under the cover of Eris' darkness?

Do you understand now
Why Ares is the defender of the weak?
Why it is always men we send into battle?

If they claim your innocence
As they claimed our birthrights,
If they can be unfaithful
To their own nature
Even now
After all they've done
In order to equate our divine gifts
To redemption...

As they return stolen traits
Reject what no longer serves them
Refuse to pay
While claiming clemency
Through a God who is forced
To protect them by true divine order...
And then they take your innocence too?

Then of course they shall be delivered to hell –

Stripped of limbs they use offensively,
Tongues of disobedience pulled
From their disdainful sneers,
Their skin disregarded
And their bones reduced
To a broth of considerable respect.

Presented to your King, in Hell,
As tokens that will serve you.

Remember, oh sweet one,
When you sit on that throne beside him
That the souls we send to you
Will protest their innocence.

It will call on your nature
To believe in the purity of them.
It will serve you
To know they are simply preserving
What little they have left.

Leave them on the battlefield.
They deserve it.

SYNONYMOUS

I wonder...
Where in your history
Did love become synonymous with pain?

AND SO THE REBIRTH BEGINS...

Maybe even
The phoenix feels fear and despair
When she surrenders.

LEAN IN

**Lean in to the longing.
It's a long road back from war.**

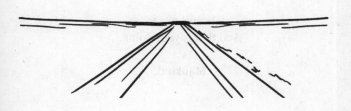

THE SACRED WHORE

They swathed me in red linens,

Painted my eyes with kohl
to cover the shadows I saw,

Painted my lips red
to prettify the truth
falling from my lips.

And you tarnished me for it.

Red, which used to be the colour
Of warmth
Of love
Of passion

Is now anger.
And that is your doing.

Mankind.

What kind of man is this?
That tarnishes Truth?

One that does not deal well
with madness.

There is a reason
madness and anger are now akin,
my love.

Can you hear that drum beat in your chest?
That thudding as you step ever closer?

The ones you tarnished are waiting
Together.
In a circle of drums
Made with the skins of men
That hid them.

And we aren't willing to prettify
Truth or madness anymore.

GRANT ME PEACE

I would happily put you through
the pain of tomorrow
If it would grant me a little peace today.

PERHAPS YOU SHOULD PRAY

Perhaps you should pray.
Looking for redemption
On that road of regret.

Perhaps those chains, that chokehold, that muzzle
Only tempered screaming nightmares.

Perhaps that's why you find Holy Communion
In the curves of a woman's body.
In a touch that terrifies you.

I play with temperance like chocolate.
Even tempered chocolate burns sweet,
Doesn't it?

Perhaps it would be better if I offer you an apple?

Perhaps you should pray.

Because screams are sweet melodies
On this road of melancholy
And you keep covering your ears,

Unwilling to listen.
Unwilling to hear.

Even the banshee's cry can be beautiful.

Perhaps you should learn the language
Of demonic love.
Of nectar, of ambrosia, of milk and honey
Wrapped in a sweet hand,
Offered to you in a careful package.

Perhaps you should
Feed your demons
What they need
Not what they crave.

Maybe then they will stop
Snapping at your heels
In starvation.

Ah... you do not yet know
What they need
Do you, my love?

Perhaps you should pray.

ICARUS' ANCESTOR

An apology
Is an inept
Excuse for you.

Like Apollo,
You are unyielding.
If I dazzle,
I am too much
Causing crows to claw your eyes
The sensation an acutely uncomfortable one
For you.

Your abandonment wound
A bedfellow in our chambers.

If I am not there,
You blame me for the cloud's arrival
And shiver in your solitude.

And if I dare
Partake and dance with the rain,
In honour of the rainbow
You dismiss me.

An awful shock.
For without me,
Your very nature withers
And dies

By your own hand.

WATER & RELEASE

Sometimes, it is only when we float alone
that we are forced to look within.
To stop abandoning ourselves, we must see
the reflection of others for what it is.

And sometimes, the strangest of people
– like an old fisherwoman – can offer
us the wisdom of time to accompany
the revelations in our own reflections.

HELD

To be able to bear you,
Embrace you,
Support the weight of you,

To be able to keep this close contact
At the speed at which we travel,

To maintain our course across the stars
Requires a tether I don't believe
either of us yet possess.

It's stomach-clenching
Stardust that implodes
And I'm reminded that even stars die.

To remain secure without breaking away.
To continue to follow a commitment
Across timelines,
my human mind cannot comprehend.

It has me slipping
Into a pool of silver mercury
Begging for mercy.

BLACKBIRDS

I see birds circling.
Blackbirds.

They've been following me
since I swam from
A past I could not outrun.

They seem to swoop
When I bring this seed
Of pomegranate to my lips.

If I feed it to them,
They'll die.

So why am I convinced
If I eat it, I'll live?

THE SIREN CALL

Let's go skinny dipping, my love.
Strip those garments of
Drama and judgement
There on the shore.

Wade into our
Crystalline waters
With intention
Or commit to deep diving.

Come, swim with Generosity
For she will give you the desires of your heart.

Our girl, Abundance,
Will amplify your experience.

Choose to swim with Love
And she'll share the secrets of the water.

Or perhaps pick Peace,
Who will wash your troubles away.

And then there is Abandon.
If you learn to swim with her

She will wash away
The need to please
The need to prove
The need to believe
You are enough.

But
A word of caution, my love.

Do not come into these waters
If you intend to fish.
For there you will find fangs.

We shall chase you
Into the depths of caves
That house the monsters
You believe are real.

If you have come seeking sanctuary
From yourself,
Then the Sirens cannot help.

ANOTHER LIFETIME

You were an insipid fool
When we last met
In Atlantis.

Unwilling to bend, even then,
In the age of rapid change.

Stood stoically by your King,
your advice that of the Sage
built on battles won
but losses forgotten.

You refused
to pay me much mind -
in public.

An upstart, you called me.
While I made moves asymmetrical to you
in a court of men and women
now lost beneath the sea.

Of course,
our battles were in private.

They still are, are they not?
Beneath skin neither one of us can touch,
beneath oceans humans dare not explore.
Both of us made now of myth, legend & fantasy.

Yet here you are,
slipping subconsciously
into my vision.

A past hallucination.

Swimming once again
in this Odyssey
with me.

REFLECTIONS

The words you chose
Individually wrapped
In barbed wire
Around that fish hook
Hanging proudly from your neck

A talisman
Cursed by its lineage
Carved as it is with protection runes

Found their mark.

I should have known better
Than to watch your mouth

When your eyes reflected
The troubled water
Zeus had waded into
For you.

SLIVERS

For a sliver of time
A mere heartbeat
The fabric of inner Earth unravels
As I float

And there is space to breathe
Through the moral fibres of my mind

Combed then slivered and spun
Into a yarn of justification

There... a story I can make sense of.

Is this how you order chaos?
By creating a space
Inside of me
That has room
To nudge a new narrative into being?

If only
By knocking down the old.

Or were you simply looking for scraps?
Stealing peeled strips of my heart
And curing them to feast on
While you searched for precious cargo?

No, it was not a careful, deliberate unpicking
Because we both know I do not possess
The patience to allow you that.

So, the former then.
To what end?

Ah, what a boring place this world would be
If it was working seamlessly.

And so the shift occurred
Internally & naturally.

ALONE

You own an island heritage I recognise
But no longer wish to inherit.

A WOMAN OF THE WORLD

A Welsh name.
A Scottish heritage.
"A woman of the world."
A lifetime split between the seas.

Alone.
Abandoned.
Ripped anew.

Desperate
for an anchor in you.

You swore to be a man the oceans would not stop.

I feel that final bind loosening
Slipping across the ocean floor
I'm worried it's going to cut itself
On that crustacean shell of yours.

A tsunami of emotions
Roll up underneath my skin

Crashing
Breaking
Retreating

Trust the wave you came in on.
Trust the timing of the tide.

After all,
It was not you
Who made your shell
Sharp enough to cut.

It was not you
Who oscillated & facilitated
The fraying of the bind.

It was me.

And now I'm anchored in
Unfamiliar familiarity

A woman of the world
Lost at sea.

What if no one else comes to love me?

THE FISHERWOMAN

Child, dry your eyes
Sip the tears from your lips.

Why are you wallowing
In such shallow waters?

Immortality leaves you
With a world to explore.

You seek me out so desperately
For skills you intrinsically know...

Intuition is the current of your mortal life.

Why do you insist on swimming against it
And drowning in your own heartache?

Take it from an old crone
A witch who fishes with Chronos,

Every time you are abandoned,
You float a little closer to home.

PERSEPHONE AND DEMETER

Written in the stars
Is another story I don't want to read
Much less acknowledge.

How can humans have so many tales
They tell themselves
For lives so short?

A life where I watched my mother
Toil for seasons
And chase the love of others

Until I believed I must work
So that the fruits of my labour
May be enjoyed
Then crinkled,
Like the crisp autumn leaves
That died by my hand.

I mistook virility
For fertility
And wondered where I lost
My femininity
Along the river of life.

I assumed my abandonment
Left death in my wake
And so I was destined
To swim along Styx.

When all along
It was your abandonment
From your mother
And hers before her
That left me questioning my worth.

THAT GOD DAMNED DINGHY BOAT

"I'll sink," he said.
"No you won't," she replied.
For that boat of hers was tried and true.

A little scuff-marked, yellow,
It buoyed at the end of the jetty
While they stood on the shore.

A god and the fisherwoman.

"You prefer solid ground underneath your feet.
But the tide of time approaches
& you are running out."

"Are you sure?" he asked.
"Certain," she said.
For that boat had taken her
To the future she had found him on.

"But it's so small."

"It has the capacity to carry you,
Do not mistake size for strength."

Gods & men tended to do that, she'd noticed.

"But the sea is rough."

"It can navigate the rapids of the river of life
With the ease of an ocean.
Do not mistake nimbleness for frailty."

Gods & men tended to do that, she'd noticed.

"It's not sturdy," he decided.

"And the sand
trickling between your toes is?" she replied.

An arched eyebrow
At a stoic God
Unwilling to acknowledge
His world was crumbling.

"Do not ignore the change of motivation
For the surety of dedication."

Gods & men tended to do that, she'd noticed.

"It is safer here," he decided.
On the steady shore he knew best.

The fisherwoman shrugged.
"If you're certain."
And then she left.

And so the god damned the dinghy boat
And the woman who taught him how to fish

For strength, agility, motivation & stability
On the shore of tomorrow
In the form of a scuffed-yellow lifeboat.

CANCER SEASON

You scuttle
Rather slowly, I might add.

Like a crab.

I think that's what makes it worse.

Must be all that armour,
That muscle mass
Makes you slow.

Juicier when broken open & cooked though.

Is this what drowning feels like?

You keep coming back
And poking holes
In my second skin.
Your pincers snap
And I can feel my heart sinking.

I can't take you home.

A watched pot never boils.
If I keep my eyes on you
Will you retreat?

If you come back,
What shall I do?

Boil you alive,
Crack your shell,
Lick the salt from your skin &
Suck the sweet marrow from your bones?

Good thing you're not a bunny.

Is this what being burned alive feels like?

I think I've made an error of judgement.
A cardinal sin.

I think I'll bathe in the holy water
Of the ocean.

NORTH NODE

My north node coils
Like the tail of a rattlesnake
Between

The Awakener
The Destroyer
&
The Expander
Of the skies.

A passionate sting
In the tale of a scorpion.

There is no peace for me.

Adventures, certainly.
Love at first sight?
With you – immediately.

But we both know this is risky territory.
For your love affairs are tempestuous at best

With quarrels and crises
And a fear of betrayal that
Once again
Binds us.

The antidote to my venom
Is to trust you to administer it.

The antidote to yours
Is to ride out the storm
I have invited you into.

I wonder if we'll survive it.

THE GOD, THE GIRL & THE FISHERWOMAN

Here is where you differ:

He would rather die of thirst
And she'd rather drown in the river.

THE SCALES OF LIBRA

Cradled in a cocoon of safety
I painted the whitewashed walls of the world
In watercolour
And claimed vibrancy.

Until it washed me under.

Emerging from the water,
Ripples began to pebble
Towards the land

And rocked the boat.

Only Calypso knows
How to tame the heart of the ocean
And when men couldn't master it
They claimed she had held them captive instead.

And so, like her,
You, too, cut off that which binds men
As if to prove you mean them no distress
No matter that it is your mere presence

And the ripples it creates
That gives them their sea legs.

As if to prove your point further
You take those binds and apply them to your skin

Tie me up
Throw me overboard
Banish the bad luck
And watch me sink back
Into the inky blackness below.

Your shadow.

Now your shadow a siren
A blaring trigger warning
A foghorn that destroys decibels of hearing

But so long as she does not break
The surface of your skin,
You can continue to believe that life is plain sailing
And that mortal men do not require saving
From the ocean you inhabit.

Oh foolish mortal,
You believe balance is an inanimate thing
Yet the mercury scales on
Your siren tail say otherwise.

You must bring to life
That which you drown to protect
In order to achieve true harmony
On the land you are desperate to inhabit.

PRACTICE

You are a practice in patience
For you have forgotten where you come from.

You are a practice in patience
Of all the things I have yet to master.

You are a practice in patience
In the virtues I claim to value
Yet do not own.

The way you test my patience
Is an impertinent practice
I long to give up.

If only I would learn it.

UNDER THE MOUNTAIN

Oh, a pattern is emerging.

A suitcase
A windowsill to the stars
A home that is not my own.

The baseline
Of where that pain began
All those years ago.

Why would she go back there?

Perhaps I am supposed to
Pursue that same path of pain
Retrace footsteps
Re-read pages
Unlock hidden knowledge
Follow a direction I didn't know to look in before.

Perhaps I am supposed to
Build stronger foundations
At the foot of the mountain
Of the woman I wish to be

Instead of the one I became.

One that is worthy of the enormity
Of our intertwined paths of passion.

But where will that lead me?
Leave us?

If homing is a beacon
An arrow pointing North
Then all paths are never-ending
And must lead within.

So here I stand
At the foot of the mountain
Ready to begin again.

EARTH & ABSENCE

When a god takes on a mortal form, they
become human in all senses of the word.

Humans are so good at getting wrapped
up in their humanity, their thoughts, their
emotions, the skin that cloaks them –
that they often forget their divinity.

In their absence from divinity,
alone with themselves,
they cannot manifest what they long for.

And when they no longer long for
it, they can manifest it.

THE FOREST OF FUTURES PAST

With the city behind me
A bridge in front of me
And a clump of trees to my right...

I turn to the pines.

Through the bristles
A hut.

In the hut
A fire.

By the fire,
A woman
Who invites me to *see*.

The flames morph
Enveloping eternity
Into one single thread of time...

And I find myself back among the pines.

Except this time, you are there with me
And our children.
One running ahead
One on your shoulders
One out of sight.

We walk through the pines
To a clearing
A waterfall
And a track to the top of the mountainside.
The view clear, but not quite spectacular.

A halfway point.

And I realise I cannot take you
To the top of the mountain with me.

It is a track for one
Treacherous & challenging
Of all my fears:

To fall from a great height
Alone.

But the view when you surpass that summit...
The view is breathtaking.

I don't stay
For views like that are supposed to be savoured
Not spoiled with excesses of time.

And so I journey back down the mountainside
To you, to the clearing, to the waterfall.
To a view that's not quite as spectacular,
But clear nonetheless.

"Did you find what you were looking for?" you ask.

I did.

And then I wait
In that clearing
While you
And our child
Our child after that
And our child after that

All make that treacherous journey
For yourselves.

Knowing that one who has already done it
Waits for you below.

A moment of time
A future that exists in a fragment
Of the forest of my mind.

HIDE

With the mentality of a hunter
Of course you still stalk in the silence.

No wonder I feel
A bristling in my bones

For the only thing that hunts
A Lioness like this
Is Man.

You hide from me
But you and I both know
It is my hide you seek

To survive in this wild world
To which you belong.

You need only ask
And I would use my teeth
As a knife

Hand my coat to you
And roam
Vulnerable
On the Serengeti
Of a soulless Earth

If it would only keep you safe.

THE WRONG SACRIFICE

How can our winter solstice last this long?

Your silence is cold
There's no hearth
There's no home.

Hestia has abandoned her post.

That altare we set
That adolere we both felt
Appears to hold
No fixed abode.

That armour you melted
Now moltenly collects
The cinders & ash
swept aside.

I worry, my love,
Mi Amor,
That we made the wrong sacrifice.

A MESSAGE FROM ERIS

Leave the earth churned up
And destruction in your wake.

Dig up that deep rich soil
That will bring new life.

Let the wound breathe,
It will heal itself naturally.

Scabs do that.

Prayers and forgiveness
Are ointment
Designed to stop infection.

But poison was not delivered here.

Hurt was.
A natural ailment of life.

Let it breathe, darling.
You have to stop believing that
destruction is a bad thing.

APPETITE

The flavour of another
Tastes strange on my tongue.

It's as if
pomegranates have permeated my taste buds.

Where you were once bold & refreshing,
The perfect balance of sweet & tart,

I find myself craving something subtle
Grounding & dark.

Like a rich coffee.

This is what happens
when you are starved for six months.

You mistake banquets for greed.

HONESTLY

You hold honesty in your mouth
Like a flavour worth savouring.

And an approach to life
That embodies heart & soul.

A temperament that tells me
You know life offers its trials

And a god's honest prayer
That is more fruitful
Than a contrived Samaritan's
Deliberate act
For proof of value.

You represent everything man could be
If only he was willing to accept
His humanity.

THE ANTIDOTE

Funny how the fever of you breaks
When one man's act of intimacy
Without trickery or expectation
Becomes an antidote
That returns me to my bones.

NOWHERE

You were nowhere to be found

Now here

Funny what a little space can do.

TYCHE'S STALEMATE

Rook
Knight
Bishop
Queen
Pawn

That is what you settled on.

A ruthless gambit
In the name of your recovery.

Men have always used me
To explain their inconsistencies
That led to unwelcome & unpleasant
Circumstances of chance.

You took vulnerability as opportunity
Intentionally or not
To tie my actions to
Ill or fair fortune for you

And like a fool, I fell for it.

So when the wheel of fortune turns
And I present you with apathy
It is because I believe you

Able to navigate a surge of uneasy change
With the ease of a captain
Who searches for cornucopia
In the harshest of seas.

For I may be blind
But I'm no fool.

The instability of your affairs
Is not my burden to bear
And the unfair absurdity
To wager that I'd find in your favour
Is precisely how Kings forfeit the game.

For everyone knows
Fortune is not found
In those final moments of victory
But in the smoothest of paths
Cut by Aphrodite.

EVERY INCH

And yet –
Every inch of my soul knows who you are.

The human half of me can't hate you –
A mathematically emotional impossibility.

NOWHERE IS WHERE YOU NEED TO GO

Remember, nowhere is a place too.

Where there's nothing left
You haven't yet experienced,
Seen or done in all the realms
Of possibility.

The epitome of tranquillity.

Certainly,
You will hunt when you hunt
Bathe when you must bathe
Love when you want to love.

But –
If you were already a King
Then you would already sit at
The top of the hierarchy
In this Patriarchal paradigm.

The only ones who
Chase, climb, scramble, toil and need
Are the ones vying for your seat.

And why would a Lioness chase a mouse
If not only for amusement?

Lionesses need to do so very little
To run a pack so very well.

It turns out, your ambition
Holds no appetite.

For men who toil and chase
Are still running from themselves.

And Queens have no desire
To mistake mice for men.

NOTHING TO STAND FOR

When you have nothing to stand for
Lying down in a six-foot grave
Makes an awful lot of sense.

DISCIPLINA

A dedicated practice.
The art of instruction
Of knowledge applied.

So when did that become
The subduing of one's bodily desires,
Obtaining something
Through the generosity
Or stealth of oneself?

When did we decide
Placing that mantle of learning
On our bodies was wise?

No wonder mortification of oneself
In any form
Breeds shame and guilt.

Perhaps it is time to strip discipline
Of its *in*-ternal affair
And take it to its origin —
Disciple.

DESIRE

Desire, true desire,
Placed in you by the Gods
And actively chased
With abandon,
Is the love of life.

It is not lust,
For it frequents the depths of your heart,
While lust merely
licks her lips and peruses
your catalogue of hopes and dreams.

Desire
is to love the life force of you.

They told you desire was bad
To be mistrusting of it
To chase love instead.

But what is mis-trusting
If not a missed opportunity of trust?

Desire is not the same as love, true.
It is, instead, equally as infinitely intrinsic,
complex and compelling.

It is as safe to trust your desires
As much as it is to love.

For desire, my dear,
exists in the depths of your soul.

It is the lifeblood through which love travels.

PERSEPHONE'S CAULDRON

In the palm of your hands
Burns the flame of who you are.

In the cauldron beyond
Desire burns away the metal
In which the world sheathed you.

Silver, liquid, mercury.

How heavy was that liquid, that armour
Now reduced to gold residue that glitters
As it settles on your skin?

A dazzling coat of brilliance.

A sun-kissed look
That tells anyone
Who looks upon you
Of the angelic nature
of your soul.

Your spark – alight
For the world to see.

A maiden turned Queen
Finally in her energy.

LESSONS

I have learnt how to navigate pain with ease
Lack of control with grace
Disagreement with decorum.

I have learnt to recognise wounds
Correct behaviours
Accept compliments.

I have learnt how to hold
Two differing experiences
In the palm of my hand

And acknowledge that both are true.

I have learnt to be a woman
Of inherent worth
In a world that told me otherwise.

I have learnt to be alone without loneliness
But have I learnt to be connected
without craving you?

Perhaps that is the next lesson.

AIR & SKIN

For man, once his purpose is known,
he must fulfil it – or die trying.
For the God of the Underworld – to
die is to fulfil his purpose.

For woman, her purpose comes once
connection is established.
From there, she creates whatever
makes her heart bloom.

This is particularly true of Persephone.

But like all maidens, she must learn
You have to have more to live for than another.
For your life, itself, is love.

Even immortals get exhausted
being human.

BEFRIENDING DEATH

If I were to die
On a desert island
I would tell you to eat the meat from my thighs.

That is the beauty of befriending death
And detaching from this mortal form.

If I were to die,
I would tell you of all the wonderful things
To expect on the other side.

I would show you how Styx's
river is slick like oil
Yet pure like water.

I would point out
Sisyphus' boulder.

In him, you would
see the human
in all

Who toil in life
Not really living
And fearing this place
Of abundant

Death.

You treat existential anxiety
Like dread
Because you cannot fathom or
Freefall into the abyss.

You do not trust what is on the other side
But, really, you do not trust yourself.
For you already know what exists.

Instead, you labour over life
The only constant you know
Fearing an inevitable end

When, really,
The quickest way
To live a life worth living
Is to treat death as an old friend.

PERSEPHONE TO HADES

I imagine chasing existential dread
While running from demons
Declared as phantoms
Is an exhausting affair.

Shall we stop?
Together?

Today, thoughts of suicide flit through my mind
Little love notes from the dead.

*It would be so very nice
to be back amongst the bones.*

Earth is tiring.
Emotions exhausting.
The separation and unity
Tug of war
The humans play
Beyond me.

Poison tastes like honey.
The abyss beckons me.

The graveyard of the souls
Left behind in grief
Haunt me
But their pain would end –
Eventually.

Oh love of mine,
Do you think they would mind
If I gifted them winter eternally?

I do so long
For my throne

In the only place
I've known as home

In the Underworld, that owns me.

HEROIN

"How would it feel right now
To drink it all away in alcohol
Or find ecstasy in heroin?"

"Honestly?
You don't want the answer
To that question."

MADNESS SEEPED IN

Madness seeped in
To crack you open
For your purpose
Was bigger
Than the mortal shell
You chose to sit in.

HADES TO PERSEPHONE

Darling, life will hold you in ways I cannot.
It will break you and shape you like clay.

But you are of Earth, so you must remain.

My Truth is not yours.

I am not seasonal or cyclic
I am an ever-present
Omnipotence.

It is the comfort of my certainty you crave.
And I will come again
Because such is your nature
That you'll invite it.

But that comfort of security
You yearn for, my love,
Is found in the cradle of feminine arms
I cannot offer
And you know it.

Life will hold you in ways I cannot.

HURRICANE

How to control a hurricane?
Do you lasso it with a noose?

Do you hunker down & hide?
Or chase it across the skies?

How do you stop a hurricane
Whose aim is pure & true?

You cannot continuously chase
A tail you cannot catch
For fear of madness.

Nor can you hide forever
And suffocate yourself to death
In a house you built.

And you cannot tighten
Your grasp around it.

It is an innocent wreckage
Leaving splintered shards of life behind
Ending in slow suicide.

But even gentle wind
Can knock you
From that pedestal
On which you stand.

You should not have used
A noose as a lasso.

MARKED

Your cold skin tinged blue tells
Of the places you have come from
Climates you've acclimated to
And where you have gone.

The missteps you have made
& the injuries you have sustained
On this road of life.

A map, a blueprint, a blanket
Wrapped around your bones

Of who you've been
& where you've come from
Of the plain you now walk
That I cannot see.

Funny then,
That you should not have seen
The marks on my heart
Of those that have met me
On this road of life

For they hold more influence
Over the person I am becoming.

Perhaps that is why all humans are lost.

Because the answers do not lie
In the past of their body
Or the future of their heart

But in the deep knowing of their bones.

GOODBYES

You always
Make it sound like such final goodbyes
Forgetting that you find me
In every lifetime.

HEARTBREAK

We should have known
This would end in heartbreak.

Yours, a reach for ecstasy, cracked open by agony
Mine, an old agony, and a
Surprising flicker of ecstasy.

THIS SINKING FEELING

I keep telling myself
the choice was out of my hands.

So why,
when I wash them
in this cracked porcelain sink,
are they covered in blue blood?

Why do I feel responsible
for being left by you
once again?

Why is there no one
I can turn to?

*Why is there no reflection
in this mirrored glass?*

DEMON FODDER

Your words are scraps,
Fodder for the demonic creature
Who has made a nest inside my head.

She tears and chews,
Rips skin with jagged teeth,
Spits it out,
And claims she is still hungry.

And you, the foolish mortal,
Continue to feed her

While she uses my bones as toothpicks.

Your well-intentioned sustenance
Is her survival...
And my downfall.

What on Earth were you thinking?

You weren't. You were speaking.
And sending me down
The river
To carry on
With Charon.

THE COUNCIL OF THE INNER WOMAN

It was blood red, the floor slick with it.
The maiden sobbing over it.
The wild woman devouring it.
The mother trying to console the maiden.
The Queen looking on.
The huntress standing beside her.
The lover playing in it.

And the wise woman knowing
What it would take

For the heart of the woman to be whole
Once more.

COMPANY TO KEEP

I needed company tonight
And you stripped even that from me.

What more could you possibly want?

Everything.
All of you.

In the darkest hours,
You whisper
"Let me die."

By morning,
You're screaming.

And I don't know what to give you.
A screaming child,
Whose understanding eludes me.

"Give me everything," you whisper.

That's what I've always done before
Until there's nothing left to give.

No stone I haven't turned

Impacted
Inspired
Loved

I've done it all.
The eulogy complete.

Why won't you let me die?
All futures are fairytales that
end in death, after all.

I sigh, because I know the answer.

You cannot tell a deathbed story
In a nursery.

And I do not wish to tell this child within me
The same sorry tales I have always told.

ATHENA TO PERSEPHONE

The lid of your skull
I lifted, and wrapped your mind
In geraniums.

MOMENTS

When I wake
- for a moment -
Before I fold into the day

I lean to fold into you
The one I slept next to

And feel my cheek kiss
Crisp white linen.
Cold, like your skin.

The memory of how you left reawakens
And I long to fall back into that blissful moment
Before reality so rudely slipped between the sheets
And took your place.

DUST ON THE WIND

Sometimes,
In the echo of your memory
I briefly return to innocence.

A sojourn through our shared experiences
Exploring possibilities of paths less travelled
In the hopes we arrive at a new destination
Together.

Essentially, all of this
is entirely meaningless.

Dust on the wind.

For our footsteps kick up old memories
And we inevitably wind up on this path.

I cannot avoid
the barricade that is the rubble of truth
sacredness is buried in.

We were never meant
To last in this lifetime.

SO SAY THE GREEK PLAYWRIGHTS

"The Gods created us to suffer through Truth."
So say the Greek playwrights.

That's what Zeus did when he paired us together,
Created a suffering like no other.

For all the best love stories
End in tragedy.

No one writes love stories
About the ones that come easy.

AND PERHAPS...

Perhaps this is what it was always supposed to be.
Perhaps that is what we agreed
Amongst the stars,
Before we came here

To Earth
With timelines of trauma
Influencing outcomes
That would catalyse
The wounds we found in one another.

You taught me to find perfection in the pain.

Perhaps that's always who you were to me.
Who we were always meant to be.

BARGAINING WITH
ANGELS

I'll make a deal, little one.
I'll finish telling you the fairytales
Of life, of love, of humans.

And when I'm done
If you still want to die,
We'll go.

Bargaining with angels.

FROM MAIDEN TO MOTHER

You, demon, made a foolish error
When you offered
To let me lie beside my babe

For I had already found gratitude
In their absence.

To assume I would so easily cave
For reconciliation
Was your mistake.

To use
One's own flesh and blood
Against them
Ignites an old, primal instinct
As ancient as Gaia herself.

Mind is made of man
But instinct... oh, she is a primal,
feral thing.
Wild like Artemis,
Bright like Apollo

Dual in her multifaceted
Diamond nature.

Your arrow missed its mark,
Caused friction
And lit a match

Awakened instincts
I thought dormant.

Perhaps
That was the purpose
Of this walkabout

Circling through
The levels of hell.

You had to know
What it would take
To push me
From Maiden to Mother

You had to know
What it would take
For me to claim
My identity

As one of Gaia's.

ANGELS

On a Tuesday morning I was musing...

What if I was God
And you were God
And everything was Perfect?

What if the pain you'd caused
The pain I'd caused
The mistakes we'd made...

All added up to this moment?

Oh, fallen angel,
I tarnished you
With the paint of pain
Coloured it in hurt
And called the artwork wrong.

When really
I should have changed the angle
Of my easel
And framed my perspective
In the gratitude of your existence.

How could I not see that life is love itself?

UNDERWORLD

And, underneath all of this, there is
a world of which you humans have
barely scratched the surface.

WHEN THE DEAD TALK

Underneath the oak tree,
With Bessie sitting next to me
And Albert next to her,
I thought about their life.

What love it would take
To be buried beside one another.

I sipped warm coffee
As blades of grass cocooned me
And I talked to the lovers
Dead long ago.

The dead make the best conversationalists.

Even you
Say more in your silence
Than you did when we were together.

And when a Screech Owl landed
In the tree
I thought of you.

And when the coffee ran cold
I thought of you.

When the winds picked up
And the blades began to scratch
I thought of you.

And when the thirst for liquor
Made my mouth water
I thought of you.

And finally,
We agreed
On something
In the silence.

You
Were an addiction
I should have never
Succumbed to

A SEAT WITH THE GODS

Where do you sit?
Amongst the gods,
So far removed from humanity
That they are but a speck?

Or do you sit in the dress circle?
Dressed in societal standards
Looking down your nose
At the carnage below?

Do you sit amongst the stalls
In the thick of it?
Where the music below you
Thrums in your blood
Where the lights above you
Dazzle your senses
Where the laughter surrounding you
Completely engulfs you?

Do you sit in the thick of it?
Humanity?

Because
Until you do
You'll never know the beauty
- *the theatre* -
of life.

That is why
The gods wanted
To walk amongst humans.

"MAMA, WHY DON'T WE GO TO CHURCH ON SUNDAYS?"

She asks me
As she sits at the kitchen counter,
Sunlight streaming through the window
Until I can see dust mites dancing in the air.

You always wanted a daughter.

God doesn't exist in the four
walls of a church, baby,
I tell her. Just like your God didn't.

He's in the warmth of your face in that sunshine,
The smell of these cookies we're baking,
The beat of the music you're swaying to.

We don't need to go to church on Sundays.
He is right here with us.

She nods, solemnly,
Like I've solved all the world's problems.

Such a wise head on such small shoulders.

"And why is God called a He?
Does that make him a boy?
Seeing as I am a She?"

No, baby.
God is a He because of
That driving force of life
That power we know of
as masculine.

"Oh...am I not powerful then?"

No, baby. You are.
For while, God is a He,
Mother Earth is a She.
Without her receptivity,
There would be nothing
To drive the power of life through.
She is what we know as the feminine.

Never forget, my darling,
You cannot spell She without He.

She nods, solemnly,
Like I've handed her a Kingdom.

Without a King.

"Mama, where is He?
Where is Daddy?"

The sunlight fades
The dust mites stop
The cookies burn
And the music cuts.

The four walls crumble
And the driving life force of You
Threatens to bring me to my knees.

Because you chose to meet your maker
Before you ever met Her.

Your daughter.

A tiny, perfect hand curls in mine.

"Don't cry Mama,
Someone told me He was with God.
I just wanted to check.
To make sure He was here with us
To bake cookies too."

EPILOGUE: MELANCHOLY

I still read the pages of our love story
Just to trace the scar across my heart.

It punctures as if I held a scalpel
And melancholy slips into my bloodstream.

Melancholy -
The origin of
Darkness made Holy.

An ink dot that stains your skin
A black hole that encapsulates everything
A midnight with no end

That is what I think of
When I think of you.

I don't think you ever saw the beauty of it
That place you existed in.

I think you saw the void as a chasm
A deep rupture in your psyche
That no one could understand.

Whereas all I saw
Was Chaos before life began.

I don't think you ever knew
The dark parts you loathed to climb out of
Were the parts I fell in love with.

I don't think you knew
You were the light in the darkness.

MELINOË

Bringer of nightmares and madness.
Daughter of Hades & Persephone.

FEMME FATALE

Book One – The Initiation of Amara:
The priestess for the humans

Book Two – The Birth of Melinoë: The
daughter of the life & death lovers

Book Three – *To be revealed in
2023: Madonna's Whore*

ACKNOWLEDGEMENTS

As always, there are people I need to thank for their help and assistance in this process, because writing a book is never a one-woman job.

Firstly, to everyone on the Instagrams who sent me messages saying they loved the random pieces of poetry I was adding to my stories. I never thought I would write a poetry book. Your encouragement was the reason I took this second book on as a book of poetry... and it has been a wild ride. I've enjoyed it so much, it's such a change of pace from novels, and it's been a skill building tool to add to my repertoire, so thank you.

Of course, this didn't come without its challenges and I also want to thank everyone who sent me messages of support in my darkest hour. Particular thanks to Erin, who gifted me the poem *Athena To Persephone*, and Amanda, who gifted me *And So The Rebirth Begins*. And to Rhiannon and Kerry, who took turns ensuring my mental health returned to its healthy state as I was finishing off the final collection of poems.

To Chelsea, the best beta reader I could ask for. I know you think you're brutal, but honestly your feedback and attention to detail make every single aspect of my books better and I could not be more grateful for you. And to Erin, once again, for being my second pair of eyes.

To Sarina, my editor. Thank you for your meticulous care and polishing of this material. These poems couldn't have been in safer hands. And to Zela for your professional approach to illustrating, and for getting it so very right even when I gave you such weak design briefs.

To Jo, for your unflinching faith in me from the beginning.

And finally, to all the readers who picked up *Prometheus' Priestess* and have joined me for this ride too, thank you. I know it wasn't quite the sequel you were expecting. I promise you'll get answers.

GWYNETH LESLEY began her writing journey when she was eight with a poem about 'Seasons' & a short story called 'Chocoholic' that featured a giant on the motorway.

She went on to write several novels and a bestselling novella under another name while she worked in London in all manner of publishing, writing & editing jobs to hone her craft.

She has also been a massage therapist, waitress & trauma support specialist... jobs she credits with making her a better author.

Gwyneth currently resides in New Zealand.

COWAN, J. C. (1897) Drawn from living action
when she was eight, with a pencil/watercolour &
... (and) worked 'freehold' that featured a place
in Launceston.

She went on to write several novels and
beautifying designs of a nature that came from an
... area in London for all manner of publications
... ing & exhibitions in to be the craft.

She has also been managing in school work as
extensive in part specialities ... both she works with
an ... for a belt... author.

... Canvas in art marks ... in New Zealand